ENHANCING ADOPTIVE PARENTING

A parenting programme for use with new adopters of challenging children

Alan Rushton and Helen Upright

Published by
British Association for Adoption & Fostering
(BAAF)
Saffron House
6-10 Kirby Street
London EC1N 8TS
www.baaf.org.uk

Charity registration 275689 (England and Wales) and SC039337 (Scotland)

© Alan Rushton and Helen Upright, 2012

British Library Cataloguing in Publication Data
A catalogue record for this book is available from the British Library

ISBN 978 1 907585 42 5

Project management by Jo Francis, BAAF
Designed by Helen Joubert Designs
Printed in Great Britain by the Lavenham Press

BAAF is the leading UK-wide membership organisation for all those concerned with adoption, fostering and child care issues.

Contents

Notes about the authors

Dr Alan Rushton spent many years as a social worker in both child and adult mental health services in the UK and in Canada. For over 25 years, he was Director of the MSc programme in Mental Health Social Work at the Institute of Psychiatry, King's College, London, where he continues as a Visiting Professor. He has been engaged in follow-up studies of older, abused children adopted from care and in predictors of placement outcome. He has published seven books, including New Parents for Older Children, Siblings in Late Permanent Placements and Adoption Support Services for Families in Difficulty. He is currently Chair of Trustees at the Post-Adoption Centre in London.

Dr Helen Upright qualified as a clinical psychologist in 1999 and initially worked within mainstream Child and Adolescent Mental Health Services. For the last eight years, she has worked as a Consultant Clinical Psychologist, heading up the Fostering and Adoption clinical psychology service for Cambridgeshire. During this time, she has provided consultation to foster carers, adopters and other professionals and run many training programmes related to the issues that adopted and fostered children face and conducted individual therapy with young people. Helen is also employed by the University of East Anglia as an Associate Tutor, teaching to the Doctorate in Clinical Psychology course.

Acknowledgements

The two original adopters' parenting manuals were devised by one of the current authors, Dr Helen Upright, Consultant Clinical Psychologist, Cambridgeshire Fostering and Adoption Clinical Psychology Service, who wrote the cognitive behavioural approach; and Mary Davidson, Adoption Adviser, Surrey County Council, who wrote the educational manual. This was in the context of the adoption support evaluation study by Professor Alan Rushton, Institute of Psychiatry, King's College London, and Dr Elizabeth Monck, Thomas Coram Research Unit, Institute of Education.

The cognitive-behavioural aspect of this programme has adopted many of the principles of behaviour management developed by Carolyn Webster-Stratton (1994) whose research has demonstrated the effectiveness of this model in reducing behaviour problems in young children. This manual uses a similar structure with additional aspects that are specific to adoptive families.

We thank the Nuffield Foundation and the Department for Education for supporting the original effectiveness trial and the Sir Halley Stewart Trust for funding this further development of the adopters' parenting manual. The views expressed in this document are those of the authors and not necessarily those of the Trust.

Peter Sandiford (CEO) and Franca Brenninkmeyer (Head of the Child and Family Service) at the Post Adoption Centre (PAC) in London helped enormously with hosting the piloting of the new manual. We are most grateful to the three parent advisers contracted to the PAC who delivered and gave feedback on the revised programme (Maggie Rogers, Esther Ina-Egbe and Kunu Gordon). Dr Danya Glaser, Consultant Child Psychiatrist, Great Ormond Street Hospital for Children, gave thoughtful advice on revising the manual, and thanks to Dr Caroline White, Consultant Clinical Psychologist, Head of the Children's and Parents' Service, Central Manchester University Hospitals Foundation NHS, for her helpful case examples.

Finally, we thank the adoptive parents who participated in this project and helped us to improve the parenting advice.

Reference

Webster-Stratton C (1994) *The Incredible Years: A troubleshooting guide for parents of children aged 3–8*, Toronto, Ontario: Umbrella Publishing

Foreword

This manual is specifically designed for professionals to use with new adopters struggling with challenging behaviour in their children. Research suggests that many adopters want to be helped in their roles, given that children adopted from care often bring extensive problems to their placements. Various studies describe adopters' needs for effective support in their efforts to introduce stability, warmth, understanding and consistency to their adopted children's lives. The manual recognises the significant challenges that can be involved and offers some practical advice. It provides the detailed content of a 10-session parenting programme. It also helpfully describes who the programme is for, indicates how practitioners should tailor it to individual family needs, advises on who should deliver the programme, and gives guidance on the knowledge and skills those professionals will need.

I have taken great interest in the development of the parenting programme, as the Academic Adviser for the Adoption Research Initiative that funded the foundations of this work (jointly with the Nuffield Foundation). The early stages of the project involved Alan Rushton and Elizabeth Monck in rigorously testing the programme's effectiveness using a randomised controlled trial (RCT). This exemplary evaluation included a comparison of the outcomes for a group of adopters who participated in the programme with those of a group who received only routine adoption support services. The results showed that there were more positive changes to parenting behaviour and progress in understanding children's problems in the group of adopters who participated in the programme. The costs of delivering the parenting programme were modest. Also, adopters who received it especially valued a regular, home-based intervention that was tailored to their specific concerns.

This RCT broke new ground. As far as I am aware, it was the first trial of a service in the adoption field in the UK. I am keen for the lessons learned to inform the commissioning of further RCTs of adoption services, given that, within the research community, trials are commonly regarded as providing the most reliable kind of evidence on the effectiveness of interventions.

With its commitment to funding innovative projects and the dissemination and implementation of research, I am delighted that the Sir Halley Stewart Trust subsequently invested in the further development, piloting and refinement of the programme.

I am now hoping that adoption agencies and adoption support agencies will promote the use of this valuable resource. Agencies can be confident that a systematic approach has been taken to its development. The intervention itself has been rigorously trialled and the test results were encouraging. Also, the learning from the original trial has been carefully integrated into the programme.

Caroline Thomas
Academic Adviser to the Adoption Research Initiative
December 2011

Research background

The initial trial and manuals

This parenting manual is written for adoption support workers and intended to make practical and relevant advice available to the many adopters struggling with challenging behaviour in their children.

Although claims are often made for the effectiveness of support services for new adopters, hard evidence of the benefits has been lacking. A range of approaches to post-placement and post-adoption support is being developed in adoption support agencies and in clinical settings but without evaluation of outcomes. This is not entirely surprising in that intervention trials in the adoption field are hard to conduct, time-consuming and demanding of financial resources. The most convincing evidence will be based on a carefully constructed trial based on comparing outcomes of those receiving the adopter parenting programme with those having only a routine support service. The essence of such a trial is that the outcome can reasonably be attributed to the parenting intervention itself while ruling out alternative explanations for changes to do with the nature of the children and their backgrounds, the adopters, the maturation of the child or other unknown factors.

Such a "real world" randomised controlled trial (RCT) was conducted by Alan Rushton and Elizabeth Monck using two training manuals – cognitive behavioural and educational – and various publications have arisen from the study describing the outcomes (Rushton and Monck, 2009; Rushton *et al*, 2010). In brief, the trial revealed that use of the training manuals was associated with increased parenting satisfaction and confidence in the adopters, although with little change in the short term in the extent of problems in the recently placed children. Those in the parenting programme, compared with those given the routine adoption support service, said they became more understanding of relationship problems with the child, more sensitive in responding to distress in the child, and gave fewer negative responses in reaction to misbehaviour. The adopters' parenting manual used in the trial was influenced by follow-up studies of late-placed children in adoptive homes which demonstrated the persistence of problems exhibited by many of the children and the challenges they presented to their adopters (Rushton *et al*, 2003; Rushton and Dance, 2006). Despite this increasing knowledge, adopters frequently find it hard to gain access to high quality, relevant, evidence-based support services which can often be marginalised in relation to other child and family services (Monck and Rushton, 2009).

Modification to the manuals

A great deal was learned both from the outcomes from the trial and from feedback from the adopters and the parent advisers on the parenting programmes. This manual is a further development of the work in order to make the programme available to a wider audience.

The two initial manuals (cognitive behavioural and educational) have been compressed into one manual, comprising a parenting programme of ten sessions, to be undertaken preferably one per week for ten weeks, on a one-on-one basis between a parent or parents, and a parent adviser. The manual now has core elements and additional sections (optional extras) for less common problems, for example, sexualised behaviour, wetting and soiling, sibling conflict, overactivity, fears and anxieties. The sequence of the manual has been revised with some sections amplified and clarified, for example, on the attachment framework.

In the original trial, feedback was obtained from the adopters and parent advisers on the strengths and weaknesses of the parenting programme. Much of this guidance has been incorporated into this revised manual. More has been added on handling aggressive behaviour and on the difficulties adopters faced in "ignoring" undesired behaviour. More attention has been paid to anticipating the child's reaction to new parenting strategies and in helping adopters to understand and respond appropriately. The programme also anticipates the possibility that adopters may get into difficulty with some strategies and further guidance on these has been included.

With the support of the Sir Halley Stewart Trust, the revised, combined manual has been tested again on six newly recruited adoptive families who have recently taken on an older child (aged 3–8) from care with serious behavioural problems. Dr Helen Upright provided training on use of the revised manual for three parent advisers during two training days. Post-intervention telephone interviews were conducted with the adopters, independently of the parent advisers. Their feedback confirmed that the combined manual worked very satisfactorily: adopters became engaged in the programme and were positive about the contents. The final revision of the manual has acknowledged the need for initial assessment of adopters' existing knowledge and skills and more tailoring of the topics to individual families' needs.

In these new cases, "before and after" questionnaires were employed, namely a parenting satisfaction scale; two child problem checklists (Assessment Checklist for Children and the Strengths and Difficulties Questionnaire); and a service user satisfaction form. Visual Analogue Scales were used to indicate emotional distress, misbehaviour and attachment behaviour in the child and the quality of relationship with the spouse/partner. These were administered to measure change in these cases, but also in the interests of developing the most salient and reliable outcome measures that could be employed in assessing the effectiveness of adopter parenting programmes in routine practice.

References

Monck E and Rushton A (2009) 'Access to post-adoption services when the child has substantial problems', *Journal of Children's Services*, 4:3, pp 21–33

Rushton A and Dance C (2006) 'The adoption of children from public care: a prospective study of outcome in adolescence', *Journal of the American Academy of Child and Adolescent Psychiatry*, 45:7, pp 877–883

Rushton A, Mayes D, Dance C and Quinton D (2003) 'Parenting late placed children: the development of new relationships and the challenge of behavioural problems', *Clinical Child Psychology and Psychiatry*, 8:3, pp 389–400

Rushton A and Monck E (2009) *Enhancing Adoptive Parenting: A test of effectiveness*, London: BAAF

Rushton A, Monck E, Leese M, McCrone P and Sharac J (2010) 'Enhancing adoptive parenting: a randomised controlled trial', *Clinical Child Psychology and Psychiatry*, 15:4, pp 529–542

Guidance on delivering the parenting programme

Aims of the parenting programme

The aims of the parenting programme are to support the stability of the adoptive placement; to reduce the level of child problems; to enhance parenting skills and understanding; and to improve relationships.

The manual combines practical parenting advice as well as help in understanding the child. It:

- offers advice on managing challenging behaviour and setting limits;
- promotes increased reflection on the child's prior experience and possible links with current behaviour and needs;
- helps adopters to maintain empathy and warmth and resist withdrawal from an unrewarding child;
- promotes calm and sensitive responding and encourages adopters to examine their own emotional responses to challenging behaviour.

A special aspect of the programme is recognising the importance for the adopters of information on the child's pre-placement history – especially any negative treatment and changes of living situation. What have adopters been told? Have they acquired a real sense of the child's prior experience? Throughout the programme, it is important to try and understand the nature of the child's behaviour and this is helped by the adopters becoming familiar with the child's early life that they have not been a part of.

The aim of the programme is to assist with current difficulties. If this proves beneficial, it is also hoped that the gains will endure beyond the intervention. However, a single, brief intervention will not suffice for all problems and may not be capable of benefiting all the children or enhancing each of the adopter's skills. Different interventions of a more intensive nature may be needed later.

The research on which this programme is based needed to recruit a highly selective sample in order to reduce the number of potentially influential factors affecting outcome. The world of practice, by contrast, has to deal with inevitable variability. Strictly, we can only be said to have evidence of effectiveness for this specific research sample (therefore not infants, adolescents, those long in placement, with severe disabilities, in special guardianship, etc). However, with this in mind, experienced practitioners should judge the relevance and suitability of each of the parenting sessions according to the individual families and the child's developmental stage.

How to use this programme

The programme has been devised and tested in relation to new adopters of children (3–8 years) displaying a high level of difficulty during the first year of placement. It is intended to be home-based, delivered by a parent adviser and involving both parents if appropriate/possible. Each session should last about 90 minutes and should be arranged at the convenience of the family and their child care routines.

The parenting programme is structured and divided into sessions in the manual, but should not be driven by a rigid menu. It covers a large amount of information, and it is recognised that if it is followed comprehensively, there may be great pressure to cover all the material in the allotted time. Therefore, the programme works best if the advice is individualised according to the families' pressing needs. The session agenda and sequence should allow for priority to be given to urgent issues. The initial session should explain that the programme has core elements and optional extras for certain problems that may only apply to some families.

The sessions are time limited (8–10 sessions). It must be clear to the adopters that the interventions will end after ten sessions and requests for continuing help will have to be referred back to the family's support worker. Carefully planned endings are therefore important as well as time for reviewing and reinforcing messages.

Handouts and summaries are provided for reinforcing important messages (e.g. children do still need to be nurtured even though they act to push the carer away). The handouts should be printed off from the CD-ROM supplied and provided to the adopters during the relevant session. Homework is set at the end of each session for the adopters to complete before the next session. Materials such as pens and paper will be needed to complete the handouts and homework.

Before beginning the programme, it is important for parent advisers to have a full overview of the child's history and to be aware of all the family members and their names, which in some cases might include birth children and other foster, adoptive or stepchildren. As the programme considers the importance of the child's pre-placement history, the parent adviser will need to negotiate access to a reliable summary of the child's pre-adoptive placement history (e.g. the Child's Permanence Report). The significance of the child's history is introduced in Sessions 1 and 2 and concerns previous moves and why they moved, relationships formed and broken, and how the child was made to feel about him/herself.

The programme is necessarily limited to parenting challenges and is not intended to cover all the varied aspects of placement support (e.g. practical, legal, financial help and contact arrangements). If the conversation strays onto a range of other topics, the adviser should politely curtail these and steer a way back to parenting issues.

Advisers will need to be aware of the adopter's developing relationship with the child. Despite the agency's initial assessment of parenting capacity, the new parent/s may respond very differently to the child once placed in their home. The nature of the parent's reactions to the new child, particularly the growth of positive feelings, and the way the child's behaviour is "read" and interpreted may be a critical feature of the early months. Finding ways of helping the parent to reflect on what is happening in the new relationship, and to maintain their warmth and their level of engagement and responsiveness with the children may be crucial.

The adopters should be assured that confidentiality will be preserved. The only reason to break this agreement would be if there were concerns about a child suffering significant harm or about the vulnerability of an adult.

Best practice when delivering the programme

- The parenting programme is designed to be delivered by experienced adoption or family workers familiar with the adoption process.

- The type and level of qualification of the parent advisers is not the key requirement. It is important that the parent advisers using this programme have the following characteristics: they need to be able to empathise with the adopters' struggles; to have good communication skills; to be able to work collaboratively with adopters; and to be able to problem solve. They need to be able to give authentic praise and encouragement.

- Parent advisers will need to be sympathetic to working jointly towards set goals in a structured programme. It is important to follow the sequence of the programme but also to balance this with being flexible when necessary. They need to convey confidence that the programme will work.

- They need to be able to build (or restore if necessary) adopters' parenting confidence. Parent advisers should receive specific training on the use of the programme: a minimum of two half-days in order to become familiar with the programme and understand its key principles. The manuals were piloted through the Post Adoption Centre in London, and training can be accessed here (Post Adoption Centre, 5 Torriano Mews, London NW5 2RZ, tel: 020 7284 0555, email: training@pac.org.uk, www.postadoptioncentre.org.uk).

- The parent advisers should be supervised and supported by a practice consultant who will also be concerned to maintain fidelity to the programme content and structure. The authors can advise on the parent adviser training and supervision.

- The attitude of the parent adviser towards the adopters is important. The aim is to empower rather than to prescribe.

- Parent advisers need to be able to assess whether the type and range of problems facing the adopters is appropriate for this programme. For example, it is designed for children with a range of serious problems, not a single isolated difficulty, nor problems of only mild difficulty.

- Parent advisers should be familiar with attachment theory, normal and abnormal child development and the profile of child problems that relate to maltreatment and insecurity.

Learning from adopters' views as service users

It is clear that the process of engagement with the adopters is extremely important. Adopters can easily be deterred from following the programme successfully if the adviser's approach is misjudged. It will be best to begin with finding out about the family and building trust and developing a relationship before moving too swiftly on to parenting strategies.

Adopters are likely to be sensitive to parenting advice being pitched at an inappropriate level. Some will be experienced parents, some will not have been parents but will have parenting/child care experience, and some will have parenting experience although it may not have prepared them for looking after ex-care children. Some will have been well prepared for parenting difficult children and others less so – or they may need reminding. The title of this programme – *Enhancing Adoptive Parenting* – implies that it is designed to build on existing skills and understanding. The parent advisers need to be able to adjust their style to adopters' experiences accordingly.

For the adopters, admitting to difficulties may run the risk of seeming to be unsuitable parents. Adopters can experience inappropriate blame if problems persist and they may feel uncomfortable about accepting help. Parent advisers should be aware of this and adjust their style of training delivery accordingly.

Introduction to understanding and managing difficult behaviour

When delivering the manual to adopters, parent advisers will be working to a sequence of structured topics, but it will be useful for them to have an up-to-date background knowledge of child development. Advisers will especially need to know about the consequences of child maltreatment (see MacMillan and Munn, 2001) child development and attachment theory to help the adopters to have a better understanding of the child's difficulties. Here, we set out some ideas to consider.

The process of distorted development

A more complex model of child development has emerged over recent years. The model applied in the field of child care practice had been very environmentalist in the past: that is, it has been concerned mostly with the adverse effects of poor or hostile parenting on children and by contrast the belief in the beneficial effects of stable, nurturing environments. However, concern has shifted somewhat in relation to the kinds of adverse events that affect development and their consequences for well-being. For instance, drug and/or alcohol abuse in pregnancy, an increasingly common phenomenon, may have adverse effects *in utero* and then persist. Furthermore, such effects often occur in combination with other factors like poor diet, smoking and the mental state of the mother. Consequently, the child born in these circumstances may already have neuro-developmental problems. The child may then have poor parenting in the early years with further negative effects on emotions and relationships – operating at both biological and psychological levels (see Glaser, 2000).

For some adopted children, difficulties may have been inherent in the child throughout. A child born with a difficult temperament is likely to be harder to care for and in some cases may evoke negative parenting behaviour, particularly if the birth parents already face several other stressors like unemployment or a lack of local/family support systems. It is sometimes the case that the "difficult" child is the last straw on the camel's back. In a minority of cases this may lead to abuse, rejection or ejection of the child from the birth family home.

The point is that the child placed for adoption may be carrying difficulties that originate from a variety of sources. For example, the presence of abuse in a child's history is likely to be highly influential on development but may not explain current behaviour by itself. Other adversities prior to the abuse; the child's characteristics (age, sex, intelligence) and response to the event (sensitivity, flexibility); subsequent insecurity; poor relationships and multiple moves in care may all accumulate and interact to produce the current problems. Therefore, suggestions that everything about the child's behaviour can be explained by a single event or circumstance should be avoided.

Distorted patterns of relating

Parent advisers should remind themselves of the key elements of attachment theory in thinking about the child's past and present carers. Attachment theory is, of course, a large and growing topic but advisers should be aware of the concepts more closely related to adoption, for example:

- the development of care seeking and exploration in infants;

- the importance of a secure base;

- parenting styles and psychological problems in parents that work against the formation of secure attachments;

- short- and long-term consequences of separation from the main care-giver;

- types of insecure attachment;

- regulations of feelings; and

- internal representations of the self and significant care-givers.

Bacon and Richardson (2001) have produced a readable but extensively referenced overview for practitioners.

Much more has been written about the development of insecure attachment than the growth of a fresh attachment with a new carer (see Hughes, 1998). There is considerable enthusiasm in some quarters for therapies to promote fresh attachment, although academic writers tend to be cautious about whether we really know what to do, what is the rationale for it and what positive effects can be expected (see O'Connor and Zeanah, 2003). It is unclear how adoptive parents contribute to the long-term course of attachment difficulties in their children although it is likely that the daily occurrences of family life over time which encourage mutual positive feelings are the most influential contributors to the development of secure attachment.

The process of developmental recovery

This parenting programme is intended to assist adopters in helping their child to achieve normal development. We were probably more optimistic 10 years ago about outcomes for abused children who were subsequently adopted, hoping that a child's natural resilience and a loving, stable home would repair the damage. Follow-up studies and clinical evidence show that, although some children do indeed make a good recovery, many children only recover slowly and some problems may persist throughout and beyond childhood. The Maudsley adoption studies have shown that children in continuing placements, even after an average of six years in the adoptive home, can still have considerable problems compared with non-adopted children (Rushton and Dance, 2006). It would, in effect, be unrealistic to think that a child loses their painful memories: their shadow at least will probably persist, and problems like "emotional dysregulation" are not likely to become "regulated" simply with change of circumstance or through short-term professional intervention (Rees, 2011).

Conveying "understanding" to adopters

What level of "understanding" should the parent advisers themselves possess? How is this "understanding" of the child's development to be conveyed by the parent advisers? It would be realistic to explain to the adopters that we by no means possess a complete understanding of the origin of problems: our theories are often inadequate and contradictory and the research evidence is so often lacking. It would be good for the parent advisers to be relieved of the burden of thinking they have to produce definitive answers as to the origin of problems. It would be more appropriate to discuss and reflect together with the adopters on how their child's puzzling behaviour might best be interpreted. In many cases, it will be useful to see a pattern of behaviour as *adaptive* in the previous abusive situation (e.g. by withdrawal, hyper-vigilance or distractibility) but which remains and is now *dysfunctional* in the new environment. As Glaser (2000) says: 'The child's developing brain is adversely affected by early negative experiences, but when the child moves to a new placement the brain doesn't know it.'

Reliable knowledge of the major pre-placement circumstances and events in the child's life should help in enhancing understanding which, in turn, should reduce the adopters' impatience, bewilderment or dashed expectations. They should, with increased insight, be able to devise parenting strategies more sensitively and rationally and to consider new approaches if the usual methods are failing.

The book *Managing Difficult Behaviour* (Pallett *et al*, 2008) covers a range of information and practical advice about child development, attachment and challenging behaviour. Although aimed at foster carers, it is also relevant for adopters. Both parent advisers and the adopters on this parenting programme may find it useful for reference.

References

Bacon H and Richardson S (2001) 'Attachment theory and child abuse: an overview of the literature for practitioners', *Child Abuse Review*, 10, pp 377–397

Glaser D (2000) 'Child abuse and neglect and the brain – a review', *Journal of Child Psychology and Psychiatry*, 41, pp 97–116

Hughes D (1998) *Building the Bonds of Attachment: Awakening love in deeply troubled children*, Northvale, NJ: Aronson

Macmillan H and Munn C (2001) 'The sequelae of child maltreatment', *Current Opinion in Psychiatry*, 14, pp 325–31

O'Connor TG and Zeanah CH (2003) 'Attachment disorders: assessment strategies and treatment approaches', *Attachment & Human Development*, 5:3, pp 223–244

Pallett C, Blackeby K, Yule W, Weissman R and Scott S (2008) *Managing Difficult Behaviour: A handbook for foster carers of the under 12s*, London: BAAF

Rees C (2011) 'All they need is love? Helping children to recover from neglect and abuse', *Archives of Disease in Childhood*, 96:10, pp 969–76

Rushton A and Dance C (2006) 'The adoption of children from public care: a prospective study of outcome in adolescence', *Journal of the American Academy of Child and Adolescent Psychiatry*, 45:7, pp 877–883

The parenting manual

Session 1: Introduction to the parenting programme

Session 2: Understanding insecurity, attachment and their effect on behaviour

Session 3: Using positive attention to change behaviour and understanding how children develop new relationships

Session 4: Special play

Session 5: Verbal praise and rewards

Session 6: Clear commands and boundaries

Session 7: Ignoring

Session 8: Effective discipline, limit setting and logical consequences

Session 9: Problem solving

Session 10: Review of the programme

Optional extras

A   Wetting and soiling

B   Sexualised behaviour

C   Managing siblings or peer relationship difficulties, disputes and jealousies

D   Regulation difficulties

E   Fears and anxieties

SESSION 1:
Introduction to the parenting programme

AIMS OF THE SESSION:

To find out about the child's history and challenging behaviours

To introduce the programme to the adopters

To discuss the adopters' expectations

To help adopters make sense of their child's difficulties

To provide a "linkage" between the past and present in regard to learning and behaviour

To explore the adopters' and their child's strategies

Brief introduction to the programme

Parent advisers should start by briefly introducing themselves to the adopters, saying a little about their experience and qualifications to begin to build up trust. They should also mention their Criminal Records Bureau clearance. As a visitor in the adopters' home, advisers must respect being a guest, but still need to make sure that the setting is right for the sessions, for example, a quiet room where there will be as little interruption as possible. The first session could begin with arranging the date and time of subsequent visits. Ideally, the sessions should take place once a week for 10 weeks. This may not always be possible, but the attempt to plan the whole sequence will help to make clear that this is a structured programme.

Briefly introduce the programme, explaining that it consists of 10 core sessions, and a number of other "optional extras". Discuss the adopters' expectations of the programme and help them to consider what they would like to gain from it.

Explain that the programme will begin by developing a psychological understanding of the child's difficulties and making sense of what impact the child's early history has had on the current level of functioning. The programme will then progress to consider a variety of evidence-based strategies the adopters can implement to help them manage their child's difficulties. It should be stressed that the behaviour management strategies in the 10 core sessions are not problem-specific, and you should try to avoid being drawn into long, repetitive discussions about one particular behaviour. The strategies discussed are designed to be used for most common behaviour problems and can be adapted accordingly. For more specific concerns, refer to the optional extras section at the end of the 10 sessions.

Explain that the programme begins in this first session with general discussion about the child and their history, their behaviour, particularly problem behaviours, and why children may behave in a certain way. You will also be discussing how the child's behaviour affects the adopters and family life, and any parenting strategies the adopters currently use.

The child's history

Continue by discussing what the adopters know about the child's pre-placement history with the birth parents (e.g. how long the child was with the birth family, why the child was removed from the birth parents, if the child has any contact with the birth family).

Are there gaps in the adopters' own learning in respect of the child's past history that may provide clues to the child's behaviour? Do they need clarification on which stages of learning the child may have missed out on? Do they need more help with understanding the effects of the identified gaps in their child's learning?

Understanding children's behaviour

Introduce the idea that parents often focus on one particular factor to explain their child's behaviour, when in fact there are often many factors. Discuss with the adopters what factors might influence their child's behaviour.

The following factors should be highlighted:

- an abusive and neglectful background

- multiple moves before coming into care and while in care

- peers and school influence

- the child's temperament and personality

- the mother's physical and mental health and drug use during pregnancy

- whether the child is particularly active

- if the child has learning difficulties

- health problems

- if the child has difficulties forming attachment relationships

- adopters' management strategies

Explain that all these factors can lead children to behave in very different ways. For example, children who have experienced abusive or neglectful backgrounds might exhibit controlling behaviour or have a tendency to be very independent. If a child has learning difficulties, this might lead them to become frustrated over their limited abilities, or if the child has difficulties forming attachments, this might lead to a child's emotional development being delayed. Such delays might cause children to exhibit rejecting behaviour towards adults as they lack the trust to be confident in developing relationships.

Highlight the importance of not getting stuck on just one factor, particularly if it is something that can't be changed. Instead, it is important to take a more global approach to thinking about their child's difficulties and to focus on the factors that *can* be altered. Encourage the adopters to identify one factor which they can quickly change to modify the child's behaviour. Indicate that the adopters' own behaviour is the easiest and quickest factor to alter in order to affect their child's behaviour.

Problem behaviours and adopters' management strategies

Ask the adopters about the child's strengths and then focus on any inappropriate behaviour the child currently exhibits. Discuss how this behaviour makes the adopters feel and what sense they make of this behaviour, explaining that there will be a return to these themes throughout the course. Discuss how the adopters currently respond to these inappropriate behaviours and what techniques have been helpful and what has not seemed to have worked.

Next, raise the possibility that, as new adoptive parents, they may have primed themselves for "major" battles – angry queries from the child about why they were removed from birth parents or foster carers, requests to "go home", the "you're not my real mum/dad" battle cry. What they probably have not been prepared for is the sheer daily grind of trying to get their child to perform the simplest of tasks, for example:

- getting ready for school on time
- locating possessions that frequently get "lost"
- eating their food too slowly
- eating their food too quickly
- sitting still whilst watching their favourite television programme.

The adopters could add to the list themselves.

It is often trivial behaviour that can be infuriating, that stops daily life from flowing smoothly and gets in the way of the bonding process. Constant reinforcement often does not seem to get results, sometimes neither does a reward system, and the child can often ultimately be viewed as simply trying to "wind them up".

What are other people's experiences of their child? Have they talked with relevant teachers and family members about problem areas?

In being asked to identify the age range of the child that they wished to adopt, was the fact that the child may be presenting as much younger explained to them? Are they making unfair comparisons with the child's peer group, children of relatives or friends? What is their understanding of the un-level playing field upon which the child is being asked to compete?

Use these discussions to help the adopters identify some **specific** goals, detailing what they would like to gain from the programme (e.g. reduce frequency of temper tantrums, increase child's ability to play).

Introduce the sequence of the programme

Explain that each session focuses on a different level of parenting, beginning with play and working up to "consequences" and "problem solving". Discuss the importance of starting with play and praise, stressing that these strategies are particularly important because they focus on developing attachment and building up positive relationships. Explain that it is only after the positive relationships have been established that the other behaviour management strategies (e.g. ignoring) will be successful in decreasing the inappropriate behaviour.

Explain that after this session, each session will follow a similar structure (starting with homework feedback, then the discussion of any new management strategy and lastly the practice of the new strategy). Tell the adopters that they will be given tasks to complete during the time between sessions and charts to fill in to keep a record of the completion of these tasks. Lastly, mention that handouts will be provided at the end of each session, which the adopters can keep and refer back to later on.

....

ANY QUESTIONS?

Ask if the adopters have any general questions about the programme.

HOMEWORK

Ask the adopters to write down what factors are important and relevant to understanding their child's behaviour. They should consider if any situations commonly trigger difficult behaviour, and also note how they respond to their child's behaviour and how their response then has an impact on their child. They should have a go at responding in different ways and note if this has an impact on the child's behaviour.

Lastly, the adopters should spend some time thinking about the information they know about their child's past. They should think in depth about how these experiences will have had an impact on how their child may view themselves and others, and consider how these views may influence their child's behaviour. For example, if their child has experienced repeated rejections, they may think of themselves as being unlovable. This in turn may lead them to be rejecting towards the adopters because they are worried about being rejected themselves.

Give out the handouts for this session.

- *Homework*
- *Things to remember: introduction to the programme*

SESSION 2:
Understanding insecurity, attachment and their effect on behaviour

AIMS OF THE SESSION:

To find out how having a child placed for adoption is working out for the new adopters

To explore what expectations they have brought to adoption

To consider what expectations the child has brought

To ask how much "baggage" there is for both the adopters and the child

To explore whether the adopters understand the nature of the task being asked of the child and of them, including assessing what preparation they have had and what level of parenting help is needed

To provide information regarding children's behaviour and attachment

Review last session and homework

Discuss with the adopters whether they have any questions about the last session.

Discuss the homework. Did they record their thoughts, feelings and behaviours about their child's behaviour? Have they noticed any patterns and whether their responses influence their child's behaviour? What factors do they think are relevant for understanding their child's behaviour?

The effects of poor early attachments

Explain that this second session will look at attachment: what attachment means, different types of attachment, the effects of poor early attachments on children, and how theories about attachment relate to individual children.

Ask the adopters to review the reliably compiled record of their child's placement history in terms of the moves they have had to make. Consider the previous placements the child has experienced and how this may have impacted on the child's ability to form new relationships and how they now view the world, for example, being distrustful of others, seeing the world as unsafe, viewing themselves as worthless. It is very likely that understanding placement history will help to make sense of their feelings of insecurity and their attachment style.

If there is a clear history of many placements and many breaks in previous attachments, ask the adopters what they are doing to convey to their child that the "here today, gone tomorrow" nature of their life so far is going to change, permanently. Discuss their existing understanding and how they would choose to reinforce "permanency".

Discuss with the adopters what knowledge they have of attachment difficulties, and continue by using the information below to increase their knowledge.

What is attachment?

- Non-clinically, it is often defined as affection, devotion, even love.

- In attachment theory, an attachment is a bond between a child and an attachment figure.

- Adults may have mutual and reciprocal attachments, but this isn't the case with child–adult relationships. This is because attachment is based on the need for safety, security and protection. In attachment theory, attachment is not synonymous with love and affection.

- It gives rise to an "internal working model" (IWM) of relationships (how a person thinks about the world) that affects interactions in adult life.

- The IWM gives the child predictability and control.

- The child develops IWMs for each attachment figure based on experiences with that person.

- IWMs are predictions which the child develops about him/herself, others and the response of others.

- People tend to view their IWMs as fact, but they can often be distorted and irrational.

Definition of attachment styles

(Developed from Mary Ainsworth's Strange Situation Procedure) A brief description of the strange situation may be necessary.

Avoidant (A) style
- During the strange situation procedure the child explores minimally while the mother is present. On separation from the mother, the child is minimally distressed, and, on being reunited with the mother the child is avoiding or ignoring.

- Likely care-giving style: not meeting child's needs, rejecting of the child.

Secure (B) style
- During the strange situation procedure, the child explores using the mother as a "secure base". On separation from the mother, the child is distressed and on being reunited with the mother, the child is quick to calm down and return to exploring the room.

- Likely care-giving style: meeting the child's needs, responding to the child's distress.

- So the child learns to trust the parent and to know that their needs will be unconditionally met.

Ambivalent (C) style

- During the strange situation procedure the child explores minimally while the mother is present. On separation from the mother, the child is extremely distressed and on being reunited with the mother, the child continues to be distressed and resists attempts to soothe.

- Likely care-giving style: not meeting the child's needs consistently.

- So children learn always to express their needs as loudly and as long as possible, as the longer they cry the more likely the mother is to meet their needs.

Disorganised (D) style

- During the strange situation procedure, the child explores minimally while the mother is present. On separation from the mother, the child continues to do nothing and on being reunited with the mother, the child does not use the mother as an attachment figure.

- Likely care-giving style: not meeting the child's needs, is unpredictable and often frightening.

- So children learn to avoid expressing their needs, and instead try to become invisible.

How attachment style influences later behaviours

Secure style
Children see themselves as worthy of love, have good self-esteem, are self-reliant, can cope with setbacks, see others as reliable, are aware that relationships involve give and take.

Avoidant style
Children see themselves as strong and independent, may have a fragile self-esteem, often emotionally distant, relate to others through practical tasks, often seen as a loner, see independence as a strength.

Ambivalent style
Children see themselves as not worthy of love, with low self-esteem, very dependent on others, often behave in "over the top" ways to get attention, over-sensitive to others' reactions, can become possessive and controlling.

Disorganised style
Children see themselves as bad, relate superficially to others, tend to get involved in abusive or abusing relationships, risk of depression and anger.

Other possible consequences of poor attachments

- Thinking problems, e.g. problems with logical thought, thinking ahead.

- Developmental problems, e.g. problems understanding others' speech, difficulties expressing themselves verbally.

- Poor conscience development, e.g. appear not to understand others' feelings, or to experience guilt.

- Problems with impulse control, e.g. poor self-control, lack of foresight, poor appreciation of danger.

- Low self-esteem.

- Relationship problems.

- Poor internal awareness, e.g. not aware of appetite, temperature.

- Tendency to be controlling in relationships.

- Poor emotional regulation.

Discuss with the adopters the idea that all of these behaviours functioned as survival strategies for children when they were in an abusive environment, e.g. avoidant children had to learn to ignore their needs and only depend on themselves, so when they move from the abusive environment, they take their "survival behaviours" with them, even though they no longer need them. Unfortunately, these behaviours are triggered most at times of stress, for example, when they move home, so at these times, they are likely to exhibit the "survival behaviours". These behaviours are no longer successful in their new environment, and are not of help to them, which makes them feel more stressed and causes them to rely on their now dysfunctional behaviours even more.

Discuss with the adopters which survival behaviours their child exhibits and how the adopters respond to these behaviours. Consider the child's early history and try to link this to the behaviours currently being exhibited. Try to develop the adopters' understanding of their child's behaviour, moving them from personalising the behaviour and blaming themselves or the child, to understanding the child's behaviour within an attachment framework.

What parents identify as infuriating behaviour specifically set up to annoy them may be the child acting out internalised thoughts and feelings which they are unable to express verbally. It is often a cry for help, but if misinterpreted can set up a cycle of parental annoyance that is difficult to break. The child may be "hard to reach" and apparently immune to even quite firm responses to misbehaviour.

Adopters should be encouraged to reflect on the "buttons" which are pressed, which could be the reasons behind this behaviour. Help them to look beyond the obvious.

Relating the attachment literature to their own child

In the light of these discussions, consider the child's behaviour and how the attachment literature enhances understanding. Also discuss the following points.

Have the adopters noted signs of progress since the child joined them? What works for the adopters and what doesn't? Does the "rest of the world" help or hinder? Have they developed a clear idea of what would help them, the child or the family?

Discuss the value of the child's past being an "open book". Do the adopters discuss it freely? Do they avoid it by being afraid of upsetting the child, or themselves? This might be short-term gain for long-term pain. Could they as adults manage a process of reinvention without so much as a backwards glance? How could the adopters encourage the child to look back to acknowledge the good and the bad?

Recognise the importance of starting with the "good" things about their child's previous families. Make a gradual introduction of talking about the "bad" things. Have the adopters done any of this? This should not only help the child come to terms with the past but should help with feelings of insecurity and "disconnectedness" from the adopters – the child has had a life that the adopters have not shared but it can become familiar through discussion.

....

ANY QUESTIONS?

Ask if the adopters have any questions about this session.

HOMEWORK

- Encourage the adopters to monitor their child's behaviour, looking out for times when they appear to make use of survival/attachment behaviours.

- Encourage the adopters to notice occasions when they personalise the child's behaviour and to remind themselves that the behaviour is more to do with the child's history rather than what is happening now.

- Encourage the adopters to look for factors that seem to improve the child's behaviour.

Give out the handouts for this session.

- *Homework and behaviour charts*
- *Attachment*
- *Things to remember about insecurity and attachment*

SESSION 3:
Using positive attention to change behaviour and understanding how children develop new relationships

AIMS OF THE SESSION:

To highlight links between adopters' beliefs about problem behaviour and parental management

To help the adopters to make links between their feelings and their child's behaviour

To help the adopters to understand the "re-invention" process that adoption requires of children

To explain why the child needs to retain the "good" aspects of their original identity and how to build them up

To understand how the child may be rationalising fears and not letting the past go

Review last session and homework

Reflect on the information provided about attachment and its impact on the adopters' understanding of their child's behaviour.

Consider whether they have noticed any factors that seem to improve their child's behaviour.

Using positive attention to change behaviour

Explain that this session will look at using positive attention to change the child's behaviour and how to develop relationships with children.

Explore with the adopters how they feel about their child's behaviour. Does the child exhibit particular problem behaviours? How do these affect the family? Help the adopters to express what is going on for them. Friends, neighbours and family members may have a similar reaction to the child's behaviour – but they will not have experienced the exhausting emotional journey that adoptive parents and children undergo.

The adopters may feel that the child who is producing disturbed behaviour is not the child they would have had. They may feel overwhelmed by the unfairness of it all – perhaps failed infertility treatment and the loss of a child, a demanding adoption process and now a child whom they find difficult to parent – this is the reality for many adopters and why the selection and assessment process for adopters is so challenging. (This may only be becoming apparent to them now.) Acknowledge the adopters' feelings about their child.

Introduce the thoughts–feelings–behaviour cycle

Move on to discuss how thoughts influence feelings and behaviour. This is an important part of the programme which introduces the necessary process of self-reflection. In particular, consider the **thoughts** the adopters have about their child and the impact these thoughts have on how they **feel** and then **behave** towards the child. Then consider how a parent's behaviour can influence a child's behaviour. Explain to the adopters how altering parents' behaviour can lead to changes in a child's behaviour.

To highlight the influence of thoughts over feelings and behaviour, discuss the following scenarios with the adopters.

Scenario 1

Imagine that it is Monday morning and pouring with rain. The gas bill has arrived, as has a reminder for your credit card repayment. Then you discover your child has spilt a sticky drink over your newly cleaned white carpet.

Ask the adopters how such a situation would make them feel, what they would think and what behaviour they might exhibit. It is likely that they will recognise that they might experience angry thoughts, feel angry and respond by shouting. Then ask the adopters to think how they would feel, what they would think and how they would behave towards the child once they have calmed down. It is likely that the parent in this situation will feel guilty, think of themselves as a bad parent and behave by trying to offer the child comfort or treats.

Ask the adopters what the child is likely to understand from these adult behaviours and what the child may learn from it (e.g. the child is likely to find the parent's behaviour very confusing and may learn to repeat the behaviour because it resulted in them receiving a reward).

Emphasise to the adopters the importance of trying to slow down the link between thought and feelings and behaviour. By slowing the cycle down it is possible to behave differently and in a more constructive way. For example, in the above scenario it is natural for a parent to feel angry and have angry thoughts, but by slowing down the link to behaviour, the parent can respond in a calm way.

Scenario 2

Imagine you give your child a hug and they push you away.

Ask the adopters how such behaviour would make them feel, what they would think and what behaviours they might exhibit. The parent in this scenario may well feel sad and think that the child does not love them, and in the long term respond by retreating from the child and gradually offering them less affection.

Consider how the parent's withdrawal of affection may then affect the child's behaviour. The child will probably retreat further from the adult, which will result in a general decrease in affection and deterioration in the relationship. Make it clear that this cycle is very common amongst children who have been through the care system. This is because their past experiences may have made them very wary of affection and relationships, so they behave in a rejecting way towards possible attachment figures.

When discussing this issue, emphasise to the adopters the importance of not getting sucked into this cycle – avoiding it by continuing to offer affection to the child, even if it feels as if none is being returned. Explore what helpful thoughts would enable the adopters to continue to provide this affection (e.g. 'My child is rejecting my affection because of their bad past experiences with close relationships, not because they do not love me').

Consider with the adopters times when their own thoughts have led them to behave in ways that have only made things worse.

Introduce the idea that children crave any type of attention

Discuss with the adopters the idea that most of a child's behaviour is aimed at gaining attention from their parents and many children want attention all the time. Even if children get 23 hours' attention a day, they will still try to get that extra hour. Point out that it is obviously impossible for any parent to provide attention to their child 24 hours a day and because of this a child learns which behaviour attracts most attention and then exhibits these behaviours most often.

Emphasise that children prefer to receive negative attention than to receive none at all (i.e. being shouted at is better than being ignored). To highlight this issue, ask the adopters what they are normally doing if their child is playing quietly in the lounge. Parents usually answer by saying that they are doing household chores. Then ask the adopters what they do if their child hits a sibling or throws a toy. The adopters are likely to say that they will rush into the room and tell the child off. Help the adopters to understand the difference between the limited attention that good behaviour generally gets and the considerable attention the child's inappropriate behaviour gains. Explain how children learn that they gain more attention by behaving badly and will therefore do so more often. Emphasise the need for the adopters to start providing attention to the positive behaviour and removing attention from the behaviour that is not appropriate.

Developing new relationships

Some adopters look forward to developing a new and satisfactory relationship with their child quickly. It may be what they have sought from adoption first and foremost. How far has this been the case for this family? How far has it been satisfied? How difficult has it been for the child who may have experienced multiple relationships? They may have viewed themselves as abandoned by parents, extended family, previous foster carers and social workers, etc – therefore what is the point in investing in a new relationship now? Experience has taught them that it won't last.

Gaining the new at the expense of the old

It may have to be pointed out to the adopters that most of us would be unwilling to enter into new relationships if it meant wiping out the past. If children are made to do so, what does that teach them about the longevity and importance of relationships – off with the old and on with the new? How can this possibly teach them how to trust? The adopters therefore need to give the child the permission and opportunity to talk about the past, revisit old haunts if security allows, reinstate links with former foster carers, old school friends, etc, if this is advisable. If not logistically possible, it can be undertaken as a paper exercise using the child's life story book and photographs.

Above all, children should be given the opportunity for discussion. They may not be very good at "talking": not all families "talk" about experiences or feelings. Many adopters will be fearful of instigating such discussion and it is unlikely the child will do so unless the right climate is created. In time, the adopters will learn to transmit the signals that say: 'This is a good moment to talk if you want to'. They will also have to "seize the moment" when the child is receptive. This could be vital therapy for the child in assisting them to move on.

Use the analogy of bereavement or divorce counselling. This is about helping people become "unstuck" and moving on, but in order for this to happen, and for them to be emotionally robust enough to form new relationships, past painful areas of failure sometimes need to be revisited. We are not suggesting formalised therapeutic sessions with their child (although in some instances this will be necessary and will need to be professionally assessed and undertaken); this is about creating a home environment in which the child can heal and grow.

Adopters need to be available to their child when she or he wants to talk about painful past experiences, but it is important to remember that there are divided views in the therapeutic world about the benefits of recalling past abuse. Therapists are becoming more cautious in the light of new research indicating that this might re-open old wounds or might re-traumatise the child. This is largely best left to mental health professionals.

Understanding the child's relationship style

Some children may initially be rejecting and withdrawn when relating to the adopters. Discuss how this makes the adopters feel and how they then respond to the child. Consider this rejecting behaviour in the context of attachment theory: for example, children who reject adult carers often have a more avoidant attachment style and are fearful of making a relationship in case they get hurt again. Many of these children adopt the attitude of "reject others before you are rejected". Again, emphasise to the adopters that the child's rejecting behaviour is not personal to the adopters, but related to the child's early history. Alternatively, some children display indiscriminate affection to parents and often to everyone they come across, for example, hugging strangers and saying 'I love you'. Sometimes, it is easy to be convinced that the child has developed a relationship quickly but more often than not, for the child, the relationship is superficial. Again, discuss how being involved in a superficial relationship can make the parent feel, and again, relate this relationship style back to attachment theory. These children are often displaying an ambivalent attachment style which keeps people at a distance.

Finding out what they are finding hard about this relationship

Identifying what the adopters are finding hard about the relationship will help them to assist the child. Are there ways they can help the child develop this relationship?

. . . .

ANY QUESTIONS?

Ask if the adopters have any questions about this session.

HOMEWORK

Ask the adopters to monitor their **thoughts** and **feelings** and to record how these affect their **behaviour**, and in turn notice how their behaviour affects their child's behaviour. Also ask the adopters to monitor to which of their child's behaviours they give attention.

Encourage the adopters to monitor how the child relates to them and other people and to begin to interpret this behaviour in terms of attachment theory.

Give out the handouts for this session.

- *Homework*
- *Parents' thought record*
- *Thoughts – feelings – behaviour cycle*
- *Things to remember about children's behaviour*

SESSION 4:
Special play

> **AIMS OF THE SESSION:**
>
> To review the last session's homework
>
> To introduce the concept of play and its importance for establishing positive relationships and effective behaviour management

Materials needed

Selection of toys for skills practice, paper and pens.

Review last session and homework

Discuss the adopters' records of their thoughts and feelings and how these affected their child's behaviour. In particular, discuss times when the adopters managed to remain calm and consider how this influenced the child's behaviour.

Also discuss the adopters' records of behaviour to which they provided most attention (i.e. the inappropriate or appropriate behaviour).

Finally, reflect on the information provided about relationships and link this to attachment theory.

Play

Explain that this session will look at the value of play, how to play most effectively with your child, and what activities may be most helpful.

Use the question, 'How often do you play with your child and do you enjoy it?', to generate discussion with the adopters.

During this discussion, highlight what kind of play activities the adopters engage in with their child and what can sometimes interfere with play. Suggest that sometimes playing with children is not enjoyable, particularly if the child is rejecting towards the parent, e.g. by avoiding eye contact or turning their back to the adult. Discuss how this rejection can make the adopters feel and normalise these feelings. Indicate that children who have been removed from their birth parents can often be rejecting during play. Discuss possible reasons for this behaviour, e.g. because the child has had little previous experience of play, or may be testing whether the adopters really want to play.

The value of play

Explore why play is important for children, for instance, in improving imagination, developing self-confidence, developing social relationships and developing attachment relationships.

Explain how this session is going to help the adopters learn a "special play" which particularly aims to develop attachment relationships. This play provides top quality, one-to-one attention to the child and is particularly good at developing attachment in children who have been neglected. Many of these children are resistant to developing close relationships (due to prior experiences) and this special play helps break down the child's barriers.

How to play

To orientate the adopters to the qualities of this play, introduce the idea of parent and child role play. Some adopters will be unfamiliar with role play and more explanation and encouragement may be necessary. You might not find it easy to conduct this in the adopters' home. If there are two adopters, they can take it in turns to be involved in each role play.

Exercise A

Tell the adopters that they are going to engage in play. The parent adviser should take the role of the parent and ask one of the adopters to play the child. During the play, the adviser should ask lots of questions, be very directive, take control and criticise a lot.

Exercise B

Tell the adopters that they are going to engage in play. The parent adviser should take the role of the parent and ask one of the adopters to play the child. During the play, the adviser should provide a running commentary, be child-led, use lots of praise and avoid asking questions.

After completing the role plays, discuss with the adopters the difference between them. Consider how each role play made the adopters feel and identify the good and bad points about the parent adviser's style of playing in each role.

From this discussion, the main rules of play should be extracted:

- use of a running commentary;
- praise;
- avoiding criticism;
- avoiding questions;
- being child-led and positive.

Ensure that the adopters have a good grasp of each principle.

- Regarding following the child's lead, ensure that the adopters are aware of the need to go at the child's pace and allow the child to make his/her own decisions during play.

- Being child-led is important because it enables the child to be in control. Explain that many children who have gone through the care system often have a strong desire to be in control (normally because it was a strategy that helped keep them safe when they lived with their birth parents). Explain that research has shown that allowing the child to be in control during play increases the likelihood of the child allowing adults to be in control during other areas of life.

- In providing a running commentary on what the child is doing, it can be helpful to liken it to a sports commentary. The running commentary is particularly important because it ensures that the parent provides 100 per cent of their attention to the child. It is this intense attention that helps build up attachment between them.

Practising play

After discussing the main rules of play, ask the adopters to practise play. Ask the adopters to act as themselves with the adviser acting as the child. Provide the adopters with specific, positive feedback for their attempts to put the play rules into practice.

What activities may be helpful?

Make clear the importance of not choosing play activities that involve the television, computer games or any learning tasks such as reading or homework, or games which may become competitive. Instead, encourage the adopters to select more creative activities, taking into account their child's age. Activities that are particularly good for increasing attachment are those which involve touch, e.g. playing with toys in the bath, having fun blowing bubbles, playing with building blocks, face painting and baking. Spend time with the adopters helping them to consider what activities their child may enjoy. Remember that it is the process of the play that is important, not the product. For example, if you bake a cake together it doesn't matter if the flour goes everywhere, what is important is that time was spent together making the cake.

Planning and homework

Ask the adopters to practise play with their child for about 10–20 minutes a day. Discuss the importance of having a regular playtime slot each day and what time would be most suitable. Emphasise that play is not conditional on the child behaving appropriately during the day and should never be withdrawn because the child has misbehaved earlier in the day. Stress that if the child has been challenging during the day, play is even more important, as it ensures that the parent and child have at least one positive interaction a day.

When the adopters start to introduce play or other positive activities, the child's behaviour may deteriorate. For example, on taking their child to the seaside for the day and having had a wonderful time, one set of parents thought they were beginning to make progress with their child. However, on the following day the child's behaviour was worse than ever, which left the parents feeling very discouraged. This pattern of behaviour is common and occurs because as these activities start to begin to build the relationship between parent and child, the child is likely to find this process anxiety provoking, so will engage in challenging behaviours to try to discourage the parent from engaging in further relationship-building activities. In these instances, the parent should be encouraged by the child's negative behaviour and continue to engage in the activities.

Acknowledge how difficult it can be for parents to play at these times. Adopters may have busy lives, rushing from one thing to the next. If they seem unable to find relaxed time with the child, it may be necessary to review the priority they give to their range of activities. Ask the adopters to keep a record of times they allocate for play.

If the child's behaviour becomes unmanageable during play, the adopters should provide a warning that the child should stop such behaviour; if the behaviour continues, then play will be stopped for that day, but resumed the day after.

. . . .

ANY QUESTIONS?

Ask if the adopters have any questions about this session.

HOMEWORK

Give out the handouts for this session.

- *Homework*
- *Special play record*
- *Things to remember about special play*

SESSION 5:
Verbal praise and rewards

AIMS OF THE SESSION:

To review the last session's homework

To introduce the concept of using praise and rewards to increase positive behaviours and develop children's self-confidence and self-esteem

To distinguish rewarding from bribing

Materials needed

Selection of toys for skills practice.

Pens and paper.

Review last session and homework

Recap the main rules of play and ask the adopters for specific examples of the play conducted. For example, discuss what the adopters played with, when and how often, how the child responded, whether the adopters enjoyed it and what got in the way of play.

If play seemed to go well and the adopters followed the main play rules, specifically praise them for the particular aspects of play that they did well – avoiding, of course, sounding patronising.

If the adopters encountered problems, first emphasise how hard this play is and praise them for the attempt despite the difficulty. Then, discuss with the adopters a particularly difficult play session. During this discussion, ask the adopters to describe, step by step, how they played and what the child did. This should help with understanding why the play was not successful and spark discussion about what the adopters could do to improve the play.

It is very useful to role play the difficult play. Encourage the adopters to act as the parents to show how they were playing. This role play will highlight which aspects of play the adopters are employing well and give opportunities for advisers to praise them. The role play also helps indicate where the adopters might not be adhering to the main rules of play. Once a clear idea has been given about where play is going wrong, recap the rules of play with the adopters. This should help them understand how they need to alter their play.

Then conduct another role play, encouraging the adopters to employ all rules of play as effectively as possible.

Introduction to the topic of praise

Ask what the adopters praise the child for and how often they praise the child. Also discuss how being able to praise the child makes the adopters feel and how their child responds to being praised.

Why is praise important?

Explain that praise is very important for children.

- It increases children's confidence and self-esteem.

- It increases appropriate behaviour.

- It develops a positive self-image.

Help the adopters to understand that you can never praise children too much, and explain that praise is good at improving the frequency of appropriate behaviour. Help the adopters understand that praising children provides them with attention for appropriate behaviour. Children are likely to repeat good behaviour so they can gain more attention.

Which behaviours should be praised?

Discuss with the adopters what behaviours they think they should praise. Discussions should ensure the adopters understand that praise should not just be given for their child's special achievements but for any behaviour that they want to be repeated.

Highlight that looking for good behaviour can be quite difficult as people can too easily focus on the negatives. To emphasise this, conduct the following exercise.

- Ask the adopters to think of five specific behaviours that they would like to see less of in their child.

- Then ask the adopters to think of five behaviours they want to see more of, making sure that these are very specific behaviours (i.e. not things like being good, doing as told, etc).

Normally, it takes people much longer to think of the good behaviours. Draw the adopters' attention to how difficult it was for them to think of good behaviours and this will highlight how hard it is to notice them. Help the adopters to recognise that if they cannot identify appropriate behaviours, then it will be difficult for the child to know how to behave.

How to make praise as effective as possible

Explain that although the adopters already praise the child, the praise must be as effective as possible. Discuss the different ways to praise and reward children.

One way is to praise verbally.

An alternative way of rewarding is to use a physical reward, e.g. healthy snacks.

Explain that both types of reward are useful and can be used to increase the frequency of appropriate behaviour. Ideally, verbal rewards should be used all the time and physical rewards should be used to increase the frequency of a particular behaviour. Explain that once the behaviour starts to appear reliably, the physical rewards can be replaced with verbal rewards. Go over the following points about increasing the effectiveness of praise.

a Be specific

Discuss with the adopters the importance of being very specific with their praise. Give examples of non-specific praise such as "great", "good boy/girl", "excellent". Discuss with the adopters how unhelpful this type of praise is because it leaves the child uncertain about what they are being praised for, and if they do not know why they are being praised, they will not repeat the behaviour. Spend time helping the adopters think of examples of specific praise (e.g. 'Well done for putting your toys away', 'That's great that you have helped to tidy your bedroom').

b Keep praise positive

Make clear that praise must be kept entirely positive. It is easy to start off being positive and then slip in a negative, for example, we may say: 'You have been such a good boy/girl today, why can't you always be like that?'. Emphasise that this negative praise diminishes the impact of praise and decreases the chance of the child repeating the appropriate behaviour. Therefore, to maintain the effectiveness of the praise, it must be kept completely positive.

c Praise behaviours in the right direction

Discuss the importance of praising children for starting a particular behaviour. For example, if children are tidying their toys, they should be praised for each toy they put away, rather than waiting for them to finish all the toys before being praised.

Discuss the following scenario with the adopters.

A child has tidied half the toys away when the mother turns to the child and says, 'Hurry up and put the rest of the toys away'.

Discuss how that child would feel, the effect the mother's comments would have on the child's behaviour, and what would have been a more effective comment for the mother to make.

d Praise immediately

Discuss the importance of praise occurring immediately after the behaviour has happened.

e Be sincere

Make it clear that all praise must be given enthusiastically and sincerely. Although this may be difficult sometimes, it is really important as children recognise when praise lacks any meaning.

Describe the following scenario to the adopters.

A child is playing, then the mother asks him/her to tidy his/her toys away as they are going shopping. The child moans and throws the toys noisily into the box.

Discuss what the mother could have said in this situation and the effect it would have on the child's behaviour (e.g. if the mother had shouted at the child for moaning, or if she had ignored the moaning and praised the child for putting the toys away).

Rejection of praise

Explain that some children reject praise, especially children who have been in the care system. For example, one child, on being told how good a drawing was, screwed it up and said it was rubbish. Discuss with the adopters why children might reject praise (e.g. they are not used to praise, they do not believe the praise, they are testing to see whether you mean the praise). Discuss how important it is to continue praising the child and emphasise that eventually the rejection will subside.

When it can be difficult to praise

At times, it may be difficult to praise. If the child has been challenging all day and then does something good, it can be difficult for parents to feel like praising. Highlight that these are probably the most important times to praise so the child can notice the difference between the attention they get when they behave well and the lack of attention they get otherwise.

Identifying specific behaviour to praise

Spend time with the adopters identifying specific behaviours they can praise. For example:

- tidying the bedroom
- putting toys away
- hanging up a coat
- laying the table
- watching TV quietly
- talking in a quiet voice
- being kind to others

Give the adopters the praise record handout and explain how they can use this to record their praise.

Appropriate physical rewards

Help the adopters develop ideas about what physical rewards to use with the child, for example, food, toys, extra TV time, extra playtime. Discuss the fact that rewards do not always have to cost money and emphasise the importance of the rewards not being expensive and being appropriate to the behaviour (e.g. not rewarding tidying the room with a new bike).

The difference between bribes and rewards

Ask the adopters the difference between bribing and rewarding.

Bribery is:

When the treat is given **before** the desired behaviour has occurred, for example, when a parent enters the supermarket and gives the child a bar of chocolate while going round the shop, hoping that this will make the child behave appropriately while shopping. Point out that bribery is unhelpful because it encourages negative behaviour: after giving the treat, there is no guarantee that the appropriate behaviour will occur and parents may end up giving further treats in the hope that the behaviour will happen at some point in the future.

A reward is:

Given **after** the child has done as required, for example, once the shopping has been completed and the child has behaved appropriately, then they may receive the treat.

It can be hard to distinguish between rewards and bribery. It is important that the adopters recognise that the behaviour must occur before the reward is given.

To check that the parent understands the concept, ask them whether the following statement is a bribe or a reward:

When you have tidied your toys then you can have a biscuit.

It is neither a bribe nor a reward: it is simply an incentive to encourage appropriate behaviour. If the child tidies the toys and is given a biscuit, it becomes a reward, however, if the parent gives the biscuit before the room is tidied, then it becomes a bribe.

Use of star charts

Ask whether the adopters have ever used star charts and if they have been successful. Spend time setting up a star chart for them to use with their child. Begin by identifying one particular behaviour for the chart to focus on. Discuss the importance of being specific about what behaviour is chosen. Discourage the adopters from having a chart for "being good" because this is too vague; equally, charts should not have too many target behaviours because it will become too complicated. Also discuss the importance of making sure that, initially, the identified behaviours are not too difficult for the child to achieve. For example, if the child never gets dressed, then the identified behaviour should be for the child to put some clothes on, rather than expecting them to get completely dressed.

Emphasise that rewards need to be small and frequent, for example, every time the behaviour occurs the child receives one star, and when they receive three stars they can have a prize. Explain that stars should never be removed, so that once a star is given it remains on the chart. Also discuss the importance of stars being given immediately after the behaviour has occurred. It is also important to remember to give the reward, as this will encourage the child to repeat the behaviour.

Explain that once the behaviour starts to occur reliably, the chart can be faded out and replaced with verbal rewards, and a new behaviour can be identified for a new star chart.

Help the adopters identify what behaviours they could tackle with the star chart. Spend time considering how the adopters can explain the star chart to the child and give them some practice at doing so by role playing this explanation, with the adopters playing themselves and the adviser playing the child.

An example of a star chart might be for the child to receive a star every time they play well with their sibling, then once they have earned three stars they get a treat. Alternatively, a "grab bag", full of inexpensive treats for the child to choose from, could be used. Whenever the adopters notice the child engaging in the desired behaviour, the child can choose a treat from the grab bag. This system is less complicated than a star chart, and therefore useful for a child who would find it difficult to achieve a number of stars to gain a reward.

ANY QUESTIONS?

Ask if the adopters have any questions about this session.

HOMEWORK

Ask the adopters to introduce the idea of a star chart to the child, to identify a particular behaviour for the chart to focus on and decide what rewards will be used. Stress the importance of the adopters continuing to use specific praise and play.

Give out the handouts for this session.

- *Homework*
- *Praise record*
- *Using verbal praise*
- *Things to remember about praise*

SESSION 6:
Clear commands and boundaries

AIMS OF THE SESSION:

To review the last session's homework

To introduce the general skills required for parents to set limits and boundaries

To help the adopters to communicate better with their children using clear commands

Review last session and homework

Discuss any successes the adopters have experienced using praise, rewards and star charts. Discuss any difficulties they encountered. The adopters should describe any problems clearly and specifically to enable solutions to be found. Check that the adopters are still playing and praising and help to find a way of solving any difficulties.

Clear commands and boundaries: introduction

Explain that this session will look at family rules and how to give commands to children in the most effective way to ensure they will be carried out.

Explain that adults give so many commands to children that it is unsurprising that most are not acted upon. Research findings have revealed that the average parent gives 17 commands every half an hour, and parents with children with behavioural problems give 40 commands every half an hour.

Discuss the adopters' thoughts about this finding, and that the research indicates that giving lots of commands does not necessarily increase a child's compliance. This is because the parent is unlikely always to enforce the child's obedience, which ultimately increases the rate of non-compliance.

Explain that children need boundaries set around their behaviour. Boundaries are important for children as they give clear messages about what behaviour is expected, help prevent children from engaging in unsafe behaviour and teach more adaptive behaviour. In addition, clear boundaries and limits provide children with a predictable and consistent framework for helping the child to develop a more trusting relationship with the parent.

Explain that encouraging compliance can be difficult, particularly with children from the care system. Many of these children have had few boundaries set round their behaviour and have experiences beyond their years.

Family rules

Family rules are a good way of increasing children's compliance. This is because eventually the rules become habits and the child will follow them without even being asked. Help the adopters to identify any rules they already have and consider what rules they could introduce, e.g. washing hands before tea, no drinks in the sitting room.

Using effective commands

Discuss the fact that the way commands are issued is also important in increasing children's compliance. Many errors made when giving commands make it easier for children not to comply.

Discuss the main principles of effective commands. For each principle, discuss whether the adopters have ever used ineffective commands and what effect they have had on their child's compliance.

a Be clear and specific

Discuss what is wrong with commands such as "Behave", "Now", "Quickly". Ensure the adopters understand that these are unhelpful because they do not clearly state what behaviour is expected. **Stress the need for commands to state clearly what behaviour is expected from the child.** For example:

I want you to wash your hands now.

b Gain the child's attention and eye contact

Discuss what happens when commands are issued before the adult has the child's full attention, e.g. shouting commands upstairs. Ensure that the adopters recognise that when commands are given without first gaining the child's attention, the child often ignores the parent. **Therefore, when commands are given the adult must first gain the child's attention.**

c Give one command at a time

Discuss the effect that giving a long list of commands has on compliance. Ensure the adopters understand that when a long list of commands is given, children are likely to forget some of the list or be so overwhelmed by the list they don't do anything on it. **Therefore, commands must be given one at a time.**

d Use a calm, firm voice

Discuss what effect shouting commands might have on children's compliance. **Therefore, commands should be given in a calm, firm voice.**

e Use child-friendly language

Explain that saying things like, 'This place is like a tip' or 'Am I the only one who does anything around here?' is unhelpful because they do not clearly state what behaviour is expected. Therefore, it is important that commands are stated using language the child can understand.

f   Use positive commands

When giving commands it is important to state what behaviour is wanted, rather than what is not wanted. For example, rather than saying, 'Stop kicking the table,' you could say, 'Keep your feet on the floor'. Or rather than, 'Don't jump in the puddle,' you could say, 'Walk around the puddle'.

g   Give short explanations

If an explanation is given about why a command should be obeyed, it should be kept short and the explanation should come first. In this way, it is the command that the child remembers.

h   Avoid using question commands

Question commands (e.g. 'Will you tidy your toys?', or 'Can you clean your teeth?') should be avoided. This is because asking children to comply gives them the option to say 'No'. **Therefore commands should be given as clear statements.**

i   When...then...commands

When...then...commands are a good way of avoiding question commands (e.g. 'When you have tidied your room, then you may watch television'). They also provide an incentive for the child to comply and they expect that the child will comply.

j   Praise compliance

Emphasise that as soon as the child starts to comply, the praise must begin.

• •

ANY QUESTIONS?

Ask if the adopters have any questions about this session.

HOMEWORK

Ask the adopters to reduce the number of commands they give to their child and make sure the commands they do give are specific.

Introduce the Commands Record and explain how to record success and difficulties with commands.

Encourage the adopters to establish some family rules, using the examples of the family rules and the family rules record.

Encourage the adopters to continue the playing and praising.

Give out the handouts for this session.

- *Homework*
- *Commands record*
- *Commands and boundaries*
- *Examples of family rules*
- *Family rules record*

SESSION 7:
Ignoring

AIMS OF THE SESSION:

To review the last session's homework

To introduce the ignoring technique to reduce inappropriate behaviour

Review last session and homework

Discuss the adopters' successful use of commands, boundaries and family rules, and problem solve any difficulties. Review the adopters' use of play, praise, clear commands and problem solve any difficulties.

Ignoring: an introduction

Discuss the adopters' prior use of ignoring. For example, consider what behaviour they have tried to ignore in the past, whether they have found ignoring effective and what makes ignoring difficult.

Why ignoring works

Explain that ignoring is useful for reducing inappropriate behaviour because it removes attention from it. Ignoring only works if the parent continues to play and praise the child. This is because the child must receive a balance between gaining positive attention for appropriate behaviour and having attention removed from inappropriate behaviour. Explain that if the adopters just ignored the child, the challenging behaviours would escalate, as the child would have no reason to behave appropriately.

Behaviour to ignore

Explore which behaviour can be ignored. Highlight that any behaviour which is inappropriate and not harmful or dangerous can be ignored, for example, moaning, crying, screaming, swearing, back chat, moodiness, irritability.

Help the adopters to identify which behaviour will be difficult to ignore. Stress that everyone finds it difficult to ignore certain behaviour as everyone varies in what irritates them the most. Children tend to work out which behaviour the parent dislikes very quickly and engage in it repetitively! For example, one adopter could manage most behaviour, except soiling. The child who came to live with her had previously displayed a range of difficult behaviour, but never soiling. A few weeks after moving in, the soiling started. This is probably because the child had engaged in various behaviours which the carer had ignored, so they had disappeared. But the adopter didn't ignore soiling so this behaviour was repeated.

The difference between ignoring and arguing

To highlight the effectiveness of ignoring, conduct the following role plays with the adopters.

Role play 1

The parent adviser should take the role of the child and one of the adopters should act as the parent.

Tell the parent that the child will ask for a biscuit and the parent should get into a discussion about whether the child can have a biscuit. Ensure that the discussion escalates into an argument.

Role play 2

Again, one of the adopters should act as the parent and the adviser as the child.

Tell the parent that the child will ask for a biscuit. Ask the parent to say to the child, 'When you have had your tea, you can have a biscuit,' and then to ignore all further comments by the child. The parent adviser will try to argue, but will quickly give up.

Discuss the difference between the two role plays, how the adopters felt in each role play, how the adopters' behaviour affected the child's behaviour, and how much attention each role play gave the child.

Principles of ignoring

Discuss the main principles of ignoring:

DON'T: Look at the child
               Speak to the child
               Touch the child

Discuss the importance of remaining calm (and looking calm) while ignoring, and how difficult this can be. Also consider the importance of using ignoring consistently, for example, by making sure the same behaviour is ignored all the time.

Explain that once the child is quiet, it is important to praise him/her for something as quickly as possible. In addition, whenever not exhibiting the problem behaviour, the child must be praised. For example, if the adopters are concerned about moodiness or sulky behaviour, then praise the child when they are being pleasant. This helps the child learn the difference between behaving inappropriately and receiving no attention and behaving appropriately and gaining attention. Say that it can be hard to praise at these times and again consider which behaviours to praise.

Warning

Make it clear that many parents find that when they first start to use ignoring, the child's behaviour can become worse before it gets better. For example, one adopter found that ignoring spitting caused it to increase. In addition, another adopter was frustrated by the child talking in a "moany" voice. Ignoring it caused the moaning to get louder and more frequent, with the child speaking in this voice most of the time. However, eventually the child gave up this voice and it disappeared altogether.

Explain that the behaviour increases because children are expecting the parent to give in and will escalate their behaviour to test whether the parent can really ignore it. Therefore, stress the importance of ignoring the inappropriate behaviour until it stops.

Increasing chances of ignoring being successful

Spend time discussing what the adopters can do to ensure that their ignoring is successful, for example, choosing a time when they are not feeling stressed (not when the child is getting ready for school). Also consider whether the adopters have relatives or friends who could be around when they first start ignoring to provide support and encouragement. Lastly, consider what distraction the adopters could employ for themselves, for example, making a cup of tea, watching TV, reading a book.

....

ANY QUESTIONS?

Ask if the adopters have any questions about this session.

HOMEWORK

Ask the adopters to begin practising ignoring and to record their attempts.

Encourage them to continuing using commands, praising and playing.

Give out the handouts for this session.

- *Homework*
- *Ignoring record*
- *Things to remember about ignoring*

SESSION 8:
Effective discipline, limit setting and logical consequences

AIMS OF THE SESSION:

To review the last session's homework

To help the adopters inform the child what behaviour is expected of him or her and what will be the consequences

To introduce consequences as an alternative strategy to manage harmful and dangerous behaviour

To address how to manage lying and stealing using consequences

Review last session and homework

Ask the adopters about successful examples of using ignoring and check that they are implementing the ignoring principles. Try to solve any difficulties they encountered with the ignoring strategies.

Review the adopters' use of commands, play, praise and rewards and try to solve any difficulties.

Limits and logical consequences

Explain that this session will look at limits and logical consequences and how to use them, including managing lying and stealing.

Ask the adopters about managing their child's most dangerous behaviour: that is, behaviour that may cause harm to others or themselves (i.e. hitting, kicking, headbanging). Discuss the disadvantages of smacking. From this discussion, compile a list of reasons for not smacking children.

Reasons should include the following.

- It teaches children that smacking is acceptable and gives a poor role model to children.

- It makes everyone upset.

- It can make children fearful.

- It rarely works in the long term as the behaviour normally recurs.

Explain that smacking has particular negative connotations for children who have been abused. For example, it can bring back traumatic memories of their previous histories and it can be rejecting. These discussions should lead to the conclusion that smacking must be avoided and alternative strategies need to be used. Such strategies include problem solving and consequences.

Introducing logical consequences

Explain that consequences are designed by the parent as punishment to fit the crime. They are best used for particularly difficult problems, e.g. not complying and dangerous behaviours, where the parent should decide before the event how to respond to a child's inappropriate behaviour. Discuss whether the adopters have any consequences currently in place with the child.

When to use logical consequences

Emphasise that the majority of children's inappropriate behaviour is not dangerous and therefore can be managed using ignoring. However, for dangerous or harmful behaviour and repeated poor compliance, then consequences can be used. Compile a list of such behaviours (e.g. hitting others, breaking things) with the adopters. It would be important to discuss the level of aggression and violence the adopters feel able to tolerate within the family home. If the adopters or other children in the household are regularly being exposed to high levels of violence, discussions should address the appropriateness of this behaviour and the viability of the placement, along with whether additional children's social services support is required.

Also, emphasise the importance of continued use of play and praise, so that the withdrawal of privileges is balanced with receiving attention for appropriate behaviour. Emphasise the importance of this balance and stress that if ignoring and consequences were the only strategies being used, then the child's behaviour would deteriorate for lack of any positive experiences.

How to use consequences

Discuss the following aspects of consequences to ensure the parent implements them appropriately.

a   Use the "If/then" rule to introduce a consequence. For example, a parent might say 'If you don't keep the noise of the TV down, then I will turn it off.'

b   Ensure the adopters have *realistic and age-appropriate expectations* of their child. For example, if children are still learning how to dress themselves, the adopters cannot expect them to do it unaided.

c   Consequences must be *fair and immediate*: delayed consequences will not have any impact on the child. For example, one could say to a child that the consequence of not working hard at school will be not being able to get a good job. This is unlikely to have an impact on the child as the consequence will not occur for many years to come. Discuss with the adopters the point that consequences need to have an immediate impact, e.g. if a child throws his or her toys during play, then they must stop playing.

d   Consequences must be *short term*. Explain that a consequence must only last a very short period of time and never longer than a few hours. Furthermore, once the consequence has been administered, the misbehaviour is no longer referred to. It can be tempting to implement more long-term consequences (e.g. grounding for a week), however, the longer a consequence lasts the less effective it becomes. Plus, to focus on negative behaviour means that opportunities for praise are being missed.

e   Make sure that the *consequences can be followed through*. Discuss with the adopters the impact of not following them through. For example, a parent might say 'If you do not go to bed on time tonight, you will go to bed early tomorrow'. When tomorrow's bedtime comes, the parent may feel bad about the consequence and allow the child to stay up. Explain that children quickly learn that their parents are likely to give in. This knowledge leads to the child rarely obeying any requests, because they know the consequences of disobedience will not occur.

f   Giving choices in advance. Discuss the importance of explaining the consequences in advance. This allows the child to be responsible for decisions to comply or otherwise. For example, the parent might say, 'If you do not play nicely with your friends, then they will have to go home.' By parents stating the consequences in this way, a child can decide what to do. Explain that giving choices in this way is particularly good for children who have been through the care system because it allows them to have some control over their decisions and their actions.

g   Consequences should not be *punitive*. For example, a parent might say, 'Because you hit me, I am going to hit you back even harder'. This is punitive and likely to make the child feel angry and retaliate later on. Such an approach may also bring back traumatic memories of when the child was in abusive situations with the birth family. Discuss with the parent how important it is to use consequences in a calm way.

h   Consequences should be *appropriate*. Explain that consequences should be appropriate to the behaviour and should not last for too long. For example, if a child draws on the wall, the parent should remove the paper and pens, only for an afternoon, not a month. It is better that consequences are short term to enable the child to learn. It will be less likely that the parent will then give in.

Managing lying and stealing

Lying and stealing are common amongst looked after and adopted children, for a variety of reasons. Consider the possible reasons for these behaviours with the adopters, ensuring the discussion covers the following factors.

- A child who has been lied to throughout their lives may not have learned that it is wrong.

- Birth parents may have encouraged the child to lie.

- Lying can serve to protect children from the awful truth.

- Some neglected children have delayed moral development, so have not learned that lying is wrong.

To manage these behaviours, discuss the following strategies.

- Do not try and get a confession out of the child. They generally won't admit to lying/ stealing, so all the parent is doing is providing attention to behaviour they want to discourage.

- Instead, the parent should simply state that they believe the child is lying/has stolen and there will now be a consequence.

- However much the child protests about this, the parent must not engage in any discussions, and should say instead that if they discover the child was telling the truth/had not stolen, then they will make amends.

- Have a discussion with the adopters about possible consequences, for example, a child who has stolen money must pay it back.

- It is also important to encourage the praising of honest behaviour.

Identify consequences

Spend time helping the adopters to identify which behaviour to use consequences for and what the consequences could be.

....

ANY QUESTIONS?

Ask if the adopters have any questions about this session.

HOMEWORK

Ask the adopters to start setting consequences and record them on the record chart.

Ask the adopters to think of a type of behaviour they want to see less of, then think of the opposite behaviour and praise their child every time the appropriate behaviour occurs.

Encourage the adopters to continue using star charts, specific praise and play.

Give out the handouts for this session.

- *Homework*

- *Consequences record*

- *Things to remember about consequences and lying/stealing*

SESSION 9:
Problem solving

AIMS OF THE SESSION:

To review the last session's homework

To ensure the adopters can help the child think of solutions to the problems and perceive which solutions are most effective

Review last session and homework

Review the adopters' successful use of consequences and problem solve any difficulties.

Discuss the adopters' continued use of play, praise and clear commands and problem solve any difficulties.

Introducing problem solving

Explain that this session will look at problem solving and how to do this with a child.

Discuss how the adopters' child tends to respond to their problems, e.g. by screaming or hitting out. Children often react in this way because they do not know any other way of responding. This is particularly true for children who have been through the care system, who are likely to have observed their own birth parents solve problems in inappropriate ways, for instance, shouting, hitting, taking drugs. Discuss how the adopters need to help the child learn more effective ways to resolve problems. These skills will provide the child with more adaptive ways of coping with difficult situations, which will help them avoid conflict and make it easier for them to maintain relationships.

Principles of problem solving

Explain that the adopters need to help the child discuss any problems they have with them. Explain that the adopters can encourage the child to discuss their problems by using the following five steps.

a Gain a specific description of the problem

Discuss the need, when a child has a problem, for the adopters to respond first by finding out more about the problem, then trying to understand the problem from the child's point of view. Adults often jump to conclusions about what the problem is and do not fully allow the child time to explain the situation. Once a clear description of the problem has been given, the adopters should spend time reflecting the problem back to the child.

b   Think of as many solutions as possible

Explain that the adopters should encourage the child to think of as many solutions as possible. Discuss the fact that it is tempting to provide children with solutions, but emphasise that children are much more likely to implement a solution which is their own idea. Also encourage the adopters to praise any attempts the child makes at offering solutions.

c   Assess the consequences of each solution

After thinking of solutions, the adopters should encourage the child to consider what would happen if each solution was carried out and then help the child assess which solution achieved the best outcome. For example, if the solution was to hit somebody, help the child consider the consequences.

d   Put the best solution into practice

Once the best solution has been decided on, discuss with the adopters how to encourage the child to implement this solution.

e   Assess the outcome

Once the solution has been implemented, the adopters can encourage the child to consider how successful the solution was by asking the following questions:

- Was the outcome harmful or dangerous to anyone?

- How did you feel about the solution and how do others feel?

Practise problem solving

Spend time helping the adopters practise problem-solving techniques using the following scenario.

Scenario

A child has come home from school upset after being told off by the teacher for hitting another child. The adviser should act the part of the child and ask one of the adopters to act as the parent. Ask the parent to follow the five-step problem-solving model (Section 3). Provide positive feedback to any of the adopters' efforts.

....

ANY QUESTIONS?

Ask if the adopters have any questions about this session.

HOMEWORK

Encourage the adopters to practise problem solving, recording their successes and difficulties.

Ask the adopters to continue playing, praising appropriate behaviour, using clear commands and ignoring inappropriate behaviour.

Give out the handouts for this session.

- *Homework*
- *Problem solving record*
- *Things to remember about problem solving*

SESSION 10:
Review of the programme

Reviewing principles and strategies

Review all the information provided about understanding the child's behaviour and all the strategies covered during the programme. Discuss with the adopters how their understanding of the child has shifted and how their thoughts about the child have altered. Help the adopters to identify why each strategy is useful and the main principles of each strategy. If the adopters encountered any difficulties, these should be problem solved. Lastly, consider the impact of all of these changes on the adopters' relationship with the child.

Give feedback

Provide the adopters with specific feedback about which area of understanding was particularly enlightening for them, and which strategies they have used particularly well, highlighting specific examples of their progress.

The importance of play and praise

At this point, it is vital to emphasise the importance of the adopters continuing to use play and praise (so that the child continues to receive attention for positive behaviour).

Bad weeks

Make it clear that the adopters may have bad days, even bad weeks, with the child. However, they should return to the handouts to check they are using all aspects of the programme.

....

ANY QUESTIONS?

Ask if the adopters have any questions about the parenting programme and what they have learned.

Give out the handouts for this session.

- *Putting it all together*

- *Things to remember*

Remind the adopters that this is the final session of the time-limited programme. There may, of course, be continuing needs which should be discussed. Further sessions could be negotiated to reinforce aspects of the programme.

OPTIONAL EXTRAS

The following five sections concern special problems that may be relevant only to some adopters. A handout for each section is available on the CD-ROM. This should be printed out and given to the adopters.

A Wetting and soiling

Introduction

Enquire whether the adopters have any concerns about the child wetting or soiling. If they do, they may want to consider engaging in this option. In this case, they should also consult their GP and consider whether the difficulties need to be investigated physically.

Outline normal toileting development

- 18 months is the earliest to consider toilet training, and two years is more realistic.

- The average child will become night trained by 33 months.

- But one in every ten five-year-olds still wets at night.

- Bear in mind that there is great variation between children, and girls develop control more quickly than boys.

Understanding why children wet and/or soil

Both wetting and soiling can be linked to underlying emotional problems. It is important for the adopters to know as much as they can about the child's toileting history prior to placement, for example, information about what degree of toileting the child has already established and whether the child experienced any regressions in toilet training at any point. This is important as it helps to reveal whether the child has ever had bladder and/or bowel control.

If the child has never had control, then it is even more important to have medical advice on the child's physical health. If there is no medical cause, it may be that the child simply does not recognise the sensation of needing to go to the toilet and/or does not know how to wipe him/herself properly. In these instances, it will be necessary to teach these skills to the child and dolls can be used to demonstrate. Wet wipes rather then dry toilet roll may be easier for the child to use. To help the child become more aware of the need to go to the toilet, the adopters should draw attention to the feeling of a full bladder or bowel. For example, they can get the child to drink a large quantity of water and to notice how their stomach feels before and after they go to the toilet.

If the child used to have control and has now lost it, then this may well be due to psychological reasons. It would be important to consider with the adopters whether the child has been exposed to any particularly stressful events recently: either a significant and obvious event, or something much more minor. Considerable thought may need to be given to explore any possible routine changes. Some children may not be aware that they need to go to the toilet and so have "accidents". Others notice they need to go, but appear not to be bothered. Others seem to engage in "revenge wetting or soiling", for example, if they have been given a consequence they may then soil their pants to show their displeasure. In some cases the child may be doing it to gain attention. Behind all of these reasons are often more complex psychological factors, such as a child's low self-esteem (thinking they are like shit) and their attempt to keep relationships at a distance (by being smelly). These factors should be discussed with the parents in an attempt to try to explain the child's toileting difficulties.

Treatment of wetting and soiling

With both difficulties, it is important that the adopters remain calm when faced with this problem. The more frustrated and irate the parent gets with the child, the more likely the child is to continue to exhibit the difficulty. Therefore, the parent must work hard to give the appearance of nonchalance when faced with wet or soiled pants. Many children will expect a negative reaction which will only serve to confirm existing negative feelings about themselves. Indicate that remaining calm is not always easy, as both soiling and wetting can give rise to many negative emotions for the parent. However, it is important that these are not displayed to the child. Discuss this issue in detail with the adopters and consider ways in which they can manage negative feelings more effectively.

Wetting

The adopters should encourage the child to engage in a regular routine of going to the toilet, particularly shortly after they have drunk something. The child should be praised even for just sitting on the toilet. Ensure that the toilet is a pleasant place to go, for example, with books and toys. Encourage the adopters to put posters up of favourite people and characters.

If the child manages to urinate in the toilet, the adopters should give considerable praise and possibly a small tangible reward. If the child wets their pants or bedsheets, the adopters should encourage the child to help clean up the mess and should respond in a calm way, providing minimum attention.

Soiling

Similarly, the adopters should encourage the child to sit on the toilet after each meal, and the child should be praised for complying. The adopters should provide a tangible reward for any success.

A child who soils should be encouraged to help clean him/herself and the soiled clothes, depending on age and ability. The idea is to encourage children to take responsibility for their actions, not to get their clothes spotless. Again, it is very important that the adopters respond calmly but in a minimal way. Soiling can lead parents to become harsh and critical of the child which tends to lead to an increase, rather than decrease, in soiling.

For both soiling and wetting, it is important that the adopters are providing positive attention and praise for other aspects of the child and their behaviour. This will help the child learn alternative ways to gain attention, and to also build their self-esteem.

B Sexualised behaviour

Introduction

Ask the adopters whether their child displays any sexualised behaviour. If they do, then discuss with them whether they would like to engage in the optional extra on sexualised behaviour.

What is "normal" sexual development and what is sexualised behaviour?

Discuss with the adopters what they think normal sexual development looks like, and what sort of behaviour causes them concern. The discussion should ensure that the adopters have a good grasp of the difference.

Normal development

- Kisses and cuddles others
- Is curious about and looks at others' body parts
- Talks about body parts
- Uses words such as "poo" and "sex"
- Plays "house" or "doctors"
- Shows, touches, or rubs own genitals
- Sometimes engages in self-soothing behaviour (masturbates)

When to be concerned

- If the behaviour becomes repetitive, excessive or hard to distract the child from, or if they are using objects to stimulate themselves (e.g. toys). Also, if the child has been masturbating so excessively that soreness results.
- If the behaviour repeatedly occurs in a public place, e.g. the living room, classroom, out shopping, even when the child has been told that this is not appropriate.
- If the child tries to touch or hurt other children in a sexual way.
- If the child shows no "stranger-danger" behaviour: for example, approaches all people and tries to engage with them, or is over-familiar with people they know slightly.

Why might a child display sexualised behaviour?

Consider with the adopters why a child might display sexualised behaviour.

Often children engage in sexualised behaviour because they have been sexually abused. By being abused in childhood, they are exposed to sensations and feelings that are beyond their years. However, once these feelings have occurred, children often continue to engage in them. Many children find that sexually stimulating themselves is soothing, and in their abusive home they may have engaged in such behaviours to soothe themselves. This behaviour then becomes entrenched, very much serving the same function as thumb sucking.

Management

Discuss the importance of managing this behaviour appropriately, getting the right balance between trying to reduce the behaviour while not leading the child to feel wrong or bad.

Encourage the adopters to try and distract the child by offering an alternative activity, and telling them that these behaviours are private and they should only engage in them in the bedroom. The child should understand that they shouldn't let anyone else touch them under their clothes and similarly, they should not touch other people. If the child has been sexually abused, and comments that someone has touched them there before, explain that this person should not have done this.

If the child is engaging in these behaviours for comfort, then it is important to teach them alternative self-soothing techniques, such as cuddling a toy, reading or drawing.

For the "stranger-danger" behaviour, it is important that this is discouraged consistently. If the child approaches a stranger or is over-familiar, the child should be stopped straight away and told that they don't know this person well, so it's not all right to talk to or touch them. In addition, the child should be rewarded whenever they don't engage in such behaviours.

It is important that family and friends support this plan. This can sometimes be difficult as people tend not to discourage small children from showing affection. However, for the child to learn safe behaviour a consistent approach is needed.

C Managing siblings or peer relationship difficulties, disputes and jealousies

Introduction

Many children with attachment difficulties find it hard to manage peer relationships. Discuss with the parents whether this is a particular concern for their child and if it is, then continue with this section.

Discuss the particular concerns of the adopters

Children who find it hard to manage peer relationships tend to fall into one of two categories:

- those who are withdrawn, socially isolated and do not interact with other children at all;

- those who can make friends initially, but gradually become bossy, controlling and possessive of their friendships, and so lose friends easily.

Consider the difficulties the child has, and try and link them back to the type of parenting they received with their birth parents.

Strategies to help children develop peer relationships

- Much of the work discussed in the emotional regulation section (D below) would be of benefit to children experiencing difficult relationships and it would be helpful to go through this section with the parent. This is because many of the peer difficulties occur due to the child's limited ability to understand their own and others' emotions.

- The adopters should provide the child with lots of opportunities to develop peer relationships, inviting other children around to play with the child, but keeping these play sessions relatively short with a clearly structured game to engage in. Keeping play sessions short will increase the chance of success. While children are playing, the adopters should ensure that the child is provided with lots of praise and encouragement when they engage in appropriate behaviour.

- Encourage the adopters to play with the child alone and to model appropriate social behaviour and to comment on and describe this behaviour to the child. During this play, the child should be prompted to display helpful behaviour and praised for doing so; for example, sharing a toy can be described and praised.

- Encourage the child to consider how their behaviour makes other children feel and the impact this may have on their friendship, considering with the child the use of more helpful behaviour. The adopters could engage the child in some pretend play using figures and dolls, or role play various different social situations, encouraging the child to guess how the figures feel.

- If the child has a tendency to be withdrawn, dolls and figures can be used to model how to start talking to someone. The adopters can play at meeting a new person first and then get the child to have a go.

- Refer back to Session 9 on problem solving; if the child is complaining of peer difficulties, the five-step problem solving approach may be useful.

- Regarding sibling rivalry, it is important for the adopters not to take sides and, for young children, to make frequent use of praise and rewards whenever one sibling engages in appropriate behaviour. A bag of small gifts is often useful, and the children can take something from the bag whenever they play well together. Generally, it is best to ignore siblings if they are arguing and to encourage the children to resolve the dispute themselves, although they will need to be directed through the resolution by the parent, for example, identifying the problem, considering each others' feelings, working through possible solutions and together choosing the best solution.

- It can also be helpful to encourage siblings to engage in tasks where they need to work together to achieve something. In this way they learn to be a team and that it is better for both of them to work together than separately – for example, to build or make something where the task will be achieved only if they both participate.

Repeating the strategies

The adopters need to be aware that these difficulties are likely to take a long time to overcome and the strategies described above need to be repeated time and time again. Also, at times of stress the child's ability to make relationships is most likely to be impaired, and so the parent needs to be aware that the child is stressed and to proactively prompt and remind the child of social skills.

D Regulation difficulties

Introduction

Discuss with the adopters the fact that that many children who have been neglected during their early years have difficulties regulating their emotions and their internal states, for example, the child may struggle to recognise their own and others' emotions, or to notice any internal cues such as hunger or temperature. If this appears to be a concern for the adopters, then consider whether they want to participate in the optional extra, 'Regulation difficulties'.

Identifying emotions

Discuss with the adopters examples of the child struggling to identify their emotions, for example, expressing all difficult emotions as anger or struggling to identify emotions in other people.

Given the child's emotional delay, the adopters will need to educate the child to recognise feelings, notice which situations commonly trigger feelings, and link them to physical sensations and to thinking about why the child may be having these feelings.

This work can be conducted gradually. Firstly, encourage the adopters to begin to increase the emotional vocabulary used with the child. It is helpful for the adopters to comment frequently on their own emotional state, and then remark on how this feeling feels physically, why they are feeling this way and what they did to resolve the feeling (if it was an unpleasant feeling).

For example, a parent could say: 'I felt really annoyed today (stating the feeling) at the supermarket, because I couldn't find anywhere to park (stating the trigger situation). I noticed my hands gripping the steering wheel and my jaw getting really tight (stating the physical sensation). I felt this way because I was in a hurry and thought I'd never park the car (stating why they felt this way). So I just had to take a deep breath and go to a different car park, where I managed to find a parking space (stating how you resolved the situation).'

Encourage the adopters to have these conversations frequently, and eventually to move on to a similar commentary about the child's emotional state.

In addition, there are numerous games the adopters can play with their child to encourage emotional development, for instance, cutting out pictures of people in magazines and trying to work out their emotions from their facial expressions and postures. The adopters can talk about how it is possible to identify the emotion, and to suggest why someone may be feeling this way. The adopters can also make "feeling cards" – cards with different emotions written on – and then use them like snap cards, or pick a card, acting out the emotion or simply pulling the facial expression so that the child has to guess what the feeling is.

Internal regulation

Similarly, many neglected children have problems identifying their internal states, for example, knowing when they are full or not or hot or cold. These can lead to various problems, particularly a tendency to overeat.

To tackle these difficulties, an approach similar to emotional regulation is needed. Encourage the adopters to increase comments on internal states, for instance, before a meal, commenting on how hungry they are, and encouraging the child to notice how empty their stomach feels. After the meal the adopters can comment on how full they feel, encouraging the child to notice the feeling of fullness. Or with temperature control, the adopters can comment on feeling cold, drawing attention to how feeling cold physically feels and that they need to put an extra layer on, or if feeling hot, describing the physical feelings of being hot (e.g. flushed face, sweating), and the conclusion that they need to take a layer of clothing off.

Some children have particular difficulties in concentrating and stopping themselves becoming over-stimulated. Such children often appear overactive and chaotic. To help these children, it is important to have a good structure and routine to daily life. It can also be helpful to have a clearly written plan for the activities or events that are due to occur throughout each day. It is important to try to educate the child about their internal feelings, so they can learn to notice when they are becoming overactive, and can divert themselves to a more calming activity. Such education is best conducted in the same way as described above. In addition, praising and rewarding the child when they manage to control themselves is also highly important.

If the child does have a tendency to overeat, it is also important to control the amount they eat, until they develop that ability themselves.

Sleep difficulties

Some neglected children have sleep difficulties, for example, nightmares, night terrors, getting out of bed frequently during the night, not going to sleep when put to bed.

There are many possible reasons for such behaviour. It may be related to the abuse the child has suffered in the birth family, or it may be the child is simply pushing the boundaries. It is also important to try to determine what the cause is before implementing any sleep programme and it may be necessary to speak to a sleep expert.

Generally, it is important to encourage the child to remain in the bedroom, even if they are not getting to sleep. It can be helpful to set up a reward system to encourage the child to remain in their room. If the child keeps coming out of their room, it is important to return them, with minimal fuss. This may need to be done repeatedly. If the child is anxious about remaining in their room, the adopters should start by sitting by the child's bed while they get ready to go to sleep and then gradually moving slowly further and further out of the bedroom and down the stairs. It may take quite a few evenings and the child will need considerable praise and rewards.

Overactivity and inattention

Some children have problems with attention, concentration and overactivity. There may be other reasons for these difficulties in addition to the attachment problems, so it is always worth the adopters discussing concerns with a mental health professional.

It is important to keep stimulation to the minimum and to try to create structure and order in the child's life, as they are likely to find this hard to do for themselves. It can be helpful to write plans with the child and encourage them to follow clear routines. It is important to reward and praise the child who does manage to attend and concentrate, even if it is just for a short period of time. It is usually best to try and break tasks down into smaller, achievable units and initially encourage the child to engage in a task only for a short period of time. Gradually, this increases the child's ability to succeed, and the length of time can slowly be extended.

E Fears and anxieties

Introduction

It is very common for all children to develop certain fears as they progress through their developmental milestones. However, children who have been abused and/or neglected may have additional fears, or some of the normal fears may become excessive. Discuss with the adopters if they have any concerns in this area, and if they do, continue with the following section.

Normal developmental fears

Most children have the overwhelming fear of being separated from their parent/s. In addition, other fears may come and go and can be of the child's own making or instilled in them by transference of anxiety from the parent.

Generally, newborn babies are startled only by sudden movement and loud noises. Then, at around six to eight months, the baby starts to become distressed if separated from the primary care-giver. At one year this continues to be problematic and babies may also react badly to loud noises. At the age of two, the fear of separation still exists, but is becoming less intense and more predictable.

Between two to four years, that obsessively tight attachment weakens further. Children are able to spend time apart from the care-giver as long as they know that the carer is nearby or easily accessible. However, in this age range new fears start to develop, such as fear of the dark and of animals. The fear of animals usually peaks at around three years of age and fear of the dark at around five years.

Between four and six years, the child develops a vivid imagination, with fear of the dark being worsened by images of ghosts and monsters. Children have fertile imaginations and are capable of developing great uneasiness as a result of hearing stories or watching television. As a result, they conjure up various visions, like ghosts, which usually disappear as they grow up.

Around six years some children start to worry about the fear of being injured and may start to worry about death.

By age ten, the child starts to experience similar worries to those seen in adulthood.

Other common fears

Baths

Most children enjoy splashing in the bath, but after the first year they may take a strong dislike to it. Sometimes even the sound of a tap running can cause them to become distressed. For some children, bathtime can trigger memories of abusive situations.

Toilets

Some children are afraid to sit on the toilet. This may be for various reasons, but is often associated with the pain of passing a particularly hard motion or the fear of being sucked into the toilet when it is flushed.

Dogs

It is common for children under four to fear animals, especially dogs.

Doctors and hospitals

From eight months, children may find medical procedures difficult and anxiety provoking, particularly if the child has experienced a painful procedure.

Additional or excessive fears

Children who have been abused and/or neglected may grow out of the fear as they develop, but the fear may be reinforced by the frightening environment in which they live. In these cases, the fear escalates and may spread to the child becoming fearful of other situations.

This is particularly true for children who have been exposed to experiences beyond their years, for example, children may have watched DVDs that feature violence or sexual acts. In addition, children who have birth parents who have been verbally or physically violent towards the child or in front of the child are also likely to have exaggerated fears. Furthermore, some children may have been told scary stories and had frightening threats made to them which will also have added to their anxieties. They may have experienced being around their birth parents when they have been very unwell, either through self-harm or drug or alcohol intake, which will have exaggerated their fears of death and dying.

Some children will be fearful of developing new significant relationships. Generally, as the child becomes more settled and secure within the placement, the fears are more readily expressed. This is because the more attached the child feels to the adopter, their fear of being rejected will become more threatening.

It is understandable that children who have been repeatedly exposed to such frightening situations are fearful. Although they are now in a safe environment, they are likely still to believe they are in danger. This fear is likely to translate into a variety of behaviours, from being clingy, to crying to angry outbursts.

It is important to try and understand the nature of the child's behaviour and this is helped by knowing as much as possible about the child's life prior to their coming to live with the adoptive parents.

Management of fears

It is most important that a child's fears are handled in a sensitive and calm manner by the parent. Although this sounds obvious, it is not always easy when the child's anxieties are expressed through anger and temper tantrums. Discuss this in detail with the adopters, and try to consider strategies they can implement to help remain calm in such circumstances.

It is also important that the adopters gain an understanding of the reasons behind the child's fear. This may be very obvious, but at other times it may require more thought. Discuss any fears the child has and try to develop an understanding of these fears with the adopters. More often than not, these fears will be rooted in their early experiences, so it will probably be helpful to try and form links between the child's fears and specific experiences in their early history.

In terms of management, it is important that the adopters are trying to be as reliable and consistent in their responses to the child as possible. If the child is exhibiting fear through crying and/or avoidance of the feared object or situation, the adopters should respond with empathy and comfort, making it clear that they understand the child's fear. It would also be helpful to try and link the child's fear to past experiences and note that these fears are no longer justified. Then it is important gradually to begin to expose the child to their fears. This should be done slowly and when the child is successful, they should be rewarded. If the child is fearful of being left alone and is clingy, the adopters should try gradually to spend longer amounts of time away from the child. This should start with a small amount of time (e.g. two minutes) and build up. To increase success, it can be helpful to give the child a clear and structured task to engage in while on their own, using a timer for the child to know when the adopter will return. When returning, the adopter should provide the child with considerable praise and positive attention.

A child expressing fear through anger should be given minimal attention at the time. However, once the chid is calm, the adopter should be empathetic and try to make links between the behaviour and the possible reasons. Again, it is important gradually to expose the child to the situation or object that they fear.

Explain to the adopters that this exposure work can be difficult, especially if the child becomes distressed. In these cases, it may be appropriate to seek professional assistance for further guidance and support.